The Revonda Factor

The Revonda Factor

BY

Noel Trowers

RoseDog Books

PITTSBURGH, PENNSYLVANIA 15222

ISBN # 0-8059-9860-8
Printed in the United States of America

First Printing

For information or to order additional books, please write:
RoseDog Books
701 Smithfield Street, Third Floor
Pittsburgh, Pennsylvania 15222
U.S.A.
1-800-834-1803

Or visit our website and online catalogue at *www.rosedogbooks.com*

Chapter One

"Searching"

1981. I was in college out-of-state. It was the loneliest year of my life. I was alone. Very much alone. I've always been somewhat of a "misfit." There was not a friend to be found anywhere. "Sociability" was never my strong point. Plus, I was struggling with my classes. I truly began to wonder why I even bothered to go to college. I needed comfort, but did not know where to find any. The following year was better. My grades picked up a bit, and I did find friendship — at least for a while. I truly hope I never experience another year like 1981 again...ever.

There was one good aspect, however, to 1981 for me. I wrote the finest songs of my life that year. Isolation does help a person to focus. Lack of distractions do inspire creativity. I don't understand how I ended up in the place in life where I am. I suppose nobody does. Life is much bigger than any of us individually. Each of us is just a very, very small part of life. Life is beyond our control. The creation, the direction of life — that's God's territory. We are too small. That is why life seems so chaotic to us at times. A person is like one piece of a jigsaw puzzle. The colors, the patterns we see often do not make any sense. God is high above us, and sees the entire puzzle in correct perspective. This is why at times the Bible seems conflicting and confusing. The conflicts and confusing details are only conflicting and confusing to us. God, the creator of life, sees it all clearly and completely. We should try to absorb and retain what we do understand and trust in God regarding the things that are beyond our comprehension.

Incidentally, I do *not* consider myself to be a religious person. However, I do believe in God and I do read the Bible. I don't think I would have survived 1981 without having a Bible to turn to. I guess I did know where to find comfort....

Life is like an ocean. Life is full of sights, sounds, rallies and rituals — from birth to death. It can be truly said, that there are a million different stories out there. Let me tell you one of them — a story from real life.

Her name was Chris, short for Christine. I will not disclose her last name so that I can freely tell you this story. Chris had posted an ad on the campus commons wall at the college where I went to. I saw the ad, and answered it. This is how we almost met. In her ad she stated she wanted to meet a nice guy to go on long walks with, perhaps take in a movie, possibly leading to a relationship. I wrote her a letter and she wrote back. This correspondence back and forth continued for a while. Chris would write about her dreams and aspirations and I would write back disclosing my goals and aspirations.

I have to mention something at this point. I am Black — African American if you prefer that term. Chris was a White female. I am not a racist, but I had to mention this because it plays a relevant component to this story. Chris did not know that I was Black. She never asked in her letters and I never brought up the subject. We just continued to write to each other, until finally the subject came up — about actually meeting each other. There was a snack shop just off campus and I agreed to meet her there at a specific date and time. I sat at the corner booth as we agreed — and waited. I waited — and waited. I thought to myself, Chris must be running a little late, but I was in no hurry so I just continued to wait. It was the day before valentine's day.

I did notice the sound of female college students just outside — laughing, gasping, and scuffling, but I paid it no mind. Finally, one of those females came inside and walked up to me. I said, "Hello — Chris?" She also said hello, but quickly stated that she was *not* Chris but one of her dorm mates.

She said her name was Julie and she came in to inform me that Chris was *not* coming in to meet me. I asked this Julie, "Why, was she ill...?" Julie sat down in the booth where I was sitting, noticeably tense, but determined to relate to me what was going on. "You see," she began, "Chris didn't know," she stopped, searching for words. "I can't believe she wouldn't even come in and say hello to you," Julie continued. "Chris literally began hyperventilating just outside the snack shop when she looked inside the door and saw you sitting there." Julie stated, "We had to rush her to the school nurse..." I was totally aghast. I didn't know all of that was going on.

Julie stated that after they walked Chris over to the school nurse's office, she felt bad that I was still sitting in the snack shop, waiting to meet Chris, oblivious as to what was going on, so she alone came back to let me know. Some people do have a conscience.

The next day I saw Julie at lunch break walking to the cafeteria and she said, "Come, sit with me at lunch" and I agreed. So I followed Julie into the cafeteria. We gathered our food trays and I followed her to a table. We sat down. I don't know why Julie sat us at the same table as Chris — directly across from her at that!

Please understand, I never met Chris so I had no idea what she looked like. Suddenly the girl sitting across from me turned beet red, and started flailing her hands around, knocking her tray, and her neighbor's drink off the table. She pushed her chair backwards, away from the table and fell to the floor!

Suddenly, everyone in the cafeteria was on their feet and several people were trying to lift this poor girl off the floor. At this point, we realized that she — Chris — was choking or strangling or something to that effect. Several people ran to get help from the college faculty. Chris was still flailing her arms and legs — still red as a beet, unable to speak a word. I could see a small amount of vomit coming out of the corners of her mouth and her nose as she thrashed about on the floor. Many hands were trying to hold her, lift her, unfortunately none of them had any rescue training. There was much cacophony and confusion going on as we waited for help.

One girl looked straight at me and said, "What did you do to her?" I blurted back, "I didn't do anything to her." Someone pulled at my shoulder and said that I "caused enough trouble" and that I should just step back. I said, "Why are you blaming me? I just sat down to eat. I said *nothing* to her! Nothing!"

The angry faces — that look. I will never forget the way they looked at me — not all of them, but many of them. The accusing glares were highly distressing.

Finally, an ambulance came and they took Chris away. Two of her friends rode with her. From what I was told it was a solid half-hour to the nearest hospital, even in the ambulance. Rural colleges are at a disadvantage there. They said Chris had "aspirated" inhaling some of her own vomit into her lungs. They said that they got her to the hospital alive, but her lungs were damaged from the gastric acid. That, and her overworked heart was a hurdle that the doctors could not overcome.

That was the beginning of that dark period in my life that was 1981. From then on most of the students steered clear of my path, because it was readily circulated through the rumor mill that I "killed" Chris. I couldn't even walk from the main academic building to the cafeteria or to the dorm without some girl complaining to the dean that I was "following" her. Once I went to the campus laundry room with a large bag to wash, and some girl named Vicki ran to the dean stating that I tried to "corner" her in the laundry room. The dean approached me and without even asking me what happened, told me to stop what I was doing or I was going to be thrown out of school. Apparently, my side of the story was not even relevant to be heard, much less considered.

And as for the cafeteria, shortly after Chris' death, I didn't even bother to go in there any more. I would get my food through a side door leading to the kitchen and eat my meals by myself in an empty room near the gymnasium. I couldn't go into the cafeteria any more because the hostility in there was so thick, you could cut it with a knife. I didn't want any more trouble so I ate my meals in that same empty room by myself for the rest of my college days.

I would see Julie in passing and she would actually stop and talk for a minute sometimes, but not much longer because she saw how people treated me and she didn't want to have the "bad eye" on her. I didn't press the issue. I didn't want any more trouble. Unfortunately sometimes trouble finds you whether you want it or not....

Life is like an ocean. And like the ocean sometimes there is much turbulence and testing. But sometimes there is calmness. Sometimes a gentle breeze comes by just to lift your spirit and give you hope.

It was 1998 when I bought my first motorcycle at thirty-six years of age. I had ridden motorbikes since I was eleven years old, but it was always "somebody else's" bike...that is, it was a rental or a borrowed motorcycle. Never my own. But at that age of thirty-six I was determined. I went to the bike dealer with one thousand dollars in my hand. So many things in life I had put aside, put down or let someone else take away from me. Not this time. I rode out on my own motorcycle that same day.

I was proud of my first motorcycle. It was not very big or powerful and it was quite old — but it ran well — and it was mine. I enjoyed riding it out to the shore. I'm not a fast rider. I just enjoy feeling the breeze. I have no interest in "testing the limits of the machine." To me, motorcycle riding is comparable to sailing.... Perhaps one day I'll buy a sailboat....

It's important to find at least one "thing" in life that you enjoy. What is that "thing?" Every person has to answer that question for themselves. When my father was alive, he told me something that I will never forget. He said, "You can have anything you want in this life — you just focus on it, and work toward it." I have found in my life that statement to be accurate. I have also found that the key word to that statement is the word "thing" - you can focus on some "thing" and work towards some "thing."

I've found that it doesn't work as well on people. You can be nice as can be to a person, but it will not cause that person to become a friend to you. A true friend is very hard to find in this life.

Love is even harder to find. In the human realm, there are so many conditions — obstacles to love that often it is impossible to reach it. Something is always wrong or not quite good enough. Love — is a tough commodity. Many people will not experience love in their lifetime, and often, despite what they may think, the obstacles blocking them from experiencing love are within themselves.

When my father was alive, he said something else that I agreed with. He said, "You know who you want to be with. If that person also wants to be with you, as for anyone else, it is truly none of their business." This is the only life you are going to live on planet earth. Live it on your terms, not someone else's. This is not an exact quote, but this is the essence of what he said — and I agree with him.

Yes, there is a place for societal concerns and social issues, but you can't let society choose the one you love. It is your life and your choice! Trust me, there is nothing sadder than a person leading a compromised life because they didn't have the backbone to stand up for the one they love — very sad. This is why some people become drug addicts or alcoholics. They are trying to fill that hole in their soul that lack of love creates.

That's why I love to ride motorcycles. Everyone needs an outlet of catharsis in their lives. It feels as though the breeze clears the thoughts of troubles out of my mind — at least for a while. However, keep in mind that not everything is for everybody. Some people cannot ride a motorcycle and some people shouldn't ride a motorcycle. You have to look at each and every aspect of life carefully and decide what outlet is right for you. Proceed with caution — through all avenues of life.

Life is like an ocean. There are many songs that have been written about the sea, or inspired by the sea — many songs that have been inspired by water. I believe this is because life originated in water, and water sustains life.

In the Book of Ecclesiastes, the writer states that "All the rivers flow to the sea." I believe this to be literally and metaphorically sound. Life is much like the waters — moving about, sometimes fast, sometimes slow, at times quietly, at other times with loud turbulence. You cannot truly understand it all. Life is too big — we are too small.

People may have their opinions, including this writer — but how much change can one lone person affect? I do believe that an individual can contribute, initiate and even inspire, but the stark reality is that they alone are just one person. Just one "little" person in a vast complicated world. And in an even bigger universe! A person is born, they live their life, hopefully they can make some positive contribution to society, and then they die. And life moves on. Others are born and the cycle continues. Read the Book of Ecclesiastes. This is not religion, this is life!

Let me tell you another story from life. Her name was Melanie. I never met her either. She lived in another part of the world. This took place around the end of 1986. I was seriously considering joining the Peace Corps. I wanted to travel to another part of the world to help those in need. While filling out papers I was presented with the idea of writing letters to someone in another part of the world — an "international correspondence club" for lack of better terms. The applicant was shown a picture and a letter written by the person in the picture, and the applicant decided which person they wanted to write back to. I sent out five letters to five different people. Melanie wrote back. Thus we began regular correspondence with each other.

I sent Melanie a picture of myself — right away. I didn't want to encounter the same problem I had with Chris back in 1981. She wrote back thanking me for sending the photo and she continued to write copiously and positively. I had found a decent job in the town where I lived, so I decided not to join the Peace Corps. However, I did want to meet Melanie, so I began to inquire about securing a tourist visa for her, which would allow her to come to the U.S. for three months. I would arrange lodging for her if she came and lodging was readily available to me at that time.

Unfortunately, this was 1986. My father emigrated to the U.S. in 1948. It was a different day and age.... In 1986, a major immigration reform act was put into place. Tourist visas were no longer being issued. This was put into place that very same year — 1986. Unbelievable! Melanie and I continued to correspond. I pursued other avenues so that we could meet. In fact, I pursued just about every other avenue that existed. Each time, I ran into a dead end. I don't know where things would have ended up for Melanie and myself, but I would have at least liked to have the chance to meet her, and to find out first hand.

Finally, I realized I could not continue to correspond with a person that I would never meet. So, I did the only thing I could. I gave her the name and address of three organizations in her country, for her country was an impoverished land. These organizations would help her with the basic necessities of life — food, clothing, housing if needed, and healthcare. I do hope all is well with her. She did write back one last time and thanked me for the information.

"Life is like an ocean. For some the ocean is just too deep, too wide, and the water is too rough. One would like to cross it — and some have crossed it successfully. But life doesn't deal everybody the same hand. Everyone should make the best of the hand that life has dealt them."

Chapter Two

"Revonda"

1994. I was still working days back then. I came home, reclined on the couch and switched on the television.

What I saw that day changed my life. It was a news flash out of Alabama. A bi-racial high school student was singled out because of her bi-racial heritage. Her school principal declared her very existence on planet earth to be a "mistake." This declaration touched off a chain reaction. As a result, that high school had two senior proms that year — one for those who supported the student and the other for those who supported the principal. Phone calls and letters poured in from all over the country. I myself was also motivated to write a letter in support of the bi-racial student.

However, my involvement did not end there. I clipped an article about this incident out of a newspaper and was holding it in my hand when I wandered into a diner for a cup of coffee. A man sat next to me at the counter and noticed the headline I was holding. He introduced himself, telling me his name was Tim Keeper and that he also was shocked and upset that an educator would condemn this poor girl's ethnicity, especially in this day and age.

It was Tim Keeper who suggested to me to start a support network for bi-racial people. It was not just lip service either. Tim Keeper, a man that I never met before, pulled forty dollars out of his wallet and handed it to me, stating that this was just his first contribution to this effort. I began writing letters to anyone or any organization, trying to raise people's awareness of bi-racial and multiracial people. Soon, people were writing me regularly.

I called this support network "Interracial Identity Correspondence." A young woman named Kathi contacted me stating that she wanted to help with the support network. She herself was bi-racial and was able to rally many family and friends to help. Interracial Identity Correspondence grew to slightly over one hundred in number in less than a year's time.

In 1996, the group participated in a large eclectic rally in Washington, D.C. Interracial Identity Correspondence was able to convince Bob Jones University in South Carolina to drop its long standing ban on interracial dating on their campus in March of the year 2000. The group also helped to change the 2000 U.S. Census, stating that because there are over six million bi-racial and multiracial people in the U.S., that they should be documented and acknowledged as such in the census tally. Interracial Identity Correspondence and many other multiracial support and advocacy entities can readily be found on the internet.

Many people still talk of people strictly in terms of Black and White — and other narrow "pigeon holes." They completely forget and disregard people like Revonda, the bi-racial high school student that we spoke about earlier in this chapter. Enough is enough! You cannot speak about people strictly in terms of Black and White because that way of thinking totally negates and disregards the existence of those "in between"... The factor that they forget about is, in fact, the factor that unites us all. I call this "The Revonda Factor," to coin a phrase. Unless each and every one of us is totally and equally considered, we will all suffer. In fact, when everyone is equally acknowledged and considered, people as a whole will benefit and prosper.

Chapter Three

✣ ✣ ✣

"Communication"

1994. That same year I had the most wonderful experience. I went on my first cruise. It was a totally positive experience. However, the best part of the whole trip was not the fine food or the top-notch activities and entertainment. It was the view from the front of the boat as we pushed further and further into the Atlantic. You couldn't see any land masses at all — just the solid blue vastness of the ocean underneath a perfectly clear sky. I felt as if I was looking directly into the glory of Heaven itself. The beauty, the serenity, the view of that expanse, will stay with me for the rest of my life.

Life is like an ocean — and the ocean is beautiful! I am just an ordinary man. I am not particularly rich, handsome or talented, but I do believe God created us all and we all have something to contribute to this world. I'm not perfect, but I know the One who is — that is — God. God loves us all. God's love doesn't differentiate or discriminate. Black, White, racial, multiracial, male, female — all created by God.

Disputes and divisions are not from God, but instead, are the result of people forgetting who God is and not giving God the highest place in their lives. God created life. God is life. God is the source of life. Religion is not God.

Religion is primarily based on tradition — not a knowledge of God.

Many religious people do not truly know who God is — and there are people who barely escaped death on 9-11-01 who are not religious, but are very close to God. Why? Because now they know what is truly important and what is not. Tragedy has a silver lining. It sets priorities straight. Tragedy helps one to clearly differentiate what's important from the trivial. The bad times in life will make a person appreciate the good times more. Make no mistake, life is good, and it is good to be alive! Enjoy the good in life and learn from the bad.

Live while you are alive! Enjoy good food and drink. Take a trip — see a place where you have never been. See how the "other side" lives. New experiences will enrich and enlighten you. In the "hustle bustle" of society, take a moment to breathe. Balance is vital to physical and emotional health. Social interaction has its place, but time alone is vital, because when one has less distractions, one can better sort out thoughts and priorities.

One has to direct one's own goals and aspirations in life. A person may "borrow a page from someone else's book," but one must never try to become a "carbon copy" of another. We are all individuals, with different thoughts, preferences and abilities.

We will not all achieve the exact same things in life. Feel free to have individual motivations and goals in life, for it is the eclecticism of life that makes it beautiful.

I encourage everyone to read the Book of Ecclesiastes. It's not very long — just twelve chapters in between Proverbs and Song of Solomon. For those not familiar with it, one will notice some familiar aspects between Ecclesiastes and this book. This is not by accident or coincidence. I've read Ecclesiastes many times and found so many parallels between it and my life. It has made an indelible impression on me.

Life itself comes from God and ultimately life is recalled by God. This is the ultimate reality.

There are many other stories I could tell you. I told you earlier about two women that I never met or spoke a word to, but who have made an impression on my life. There are many other stories that I could tell you, but it is nothing new. Many people can tell you stories about the "drama and tragedies" of life. This is nothing new — "nothing new under the sun." We've all had good and bad experiences in life. Some have had it worse than others. So, I feel despite all, I shouldn't complain.

God is good and God is good to me. I have a picture that I keep in my file of a disabled war veteran. He has no legs and only one arm. But in the picture, he has the biggest smile on his face. So I wrote a note on the bottom of the picture to encourage myself — "See, it could be worse."

We must not take anything for granted in life. Today I may walk along the seashore. Tomorrow something could happen to me and I may not be able to walk at all. Thank God for even the most basic aspects of life! Again I emphasize, this is not religion — this is life — this is truth — ultimate reality. Thank God for it all.

Revonda, the bi-racial student, is another woman who I never met or spoke to but who has made an impression on my life. When I saw her story on television, it affected me deeply. It is not a "racial" or "interracial" issue — it's a *human* issue. It doesn't matter if you are Black, White, Asian, Bi-racial, Multiracial, whatever. You are a human being and nothing in our ethnic make-up makes us any better or worse than anybody else. God created us all.

The fact that there are bi-racial and multiracial people in existence, proves that interracial inter-relations do not violate any natural order of God. In other words, those who advocate separatism are advocating a human "hang-up".... Simply put — racial issues are people's issues — not God's issues. God created us all, including bi-racial people like Revonda. It is arrogant, out of place, and simply wrong to make someone like Revonda feel inferior about their ethnic make-up. Bi-racial people are just people — no worse or any better than anybody else.

It is important that everybody respects everybody. At the same time, let us as a society endeavor to push past racial issues. There is so much more to life. I enjoy music - do you? I enjoy a good meal and a refreshing drink. I don't always talk about "issues." I want to enjoy life, and I would suggest to anyone reading this, to do the same. I love the shore. Some people enjoy the mountains. What's your pleasure? It is better to say, "I'm glad I did" instead of "I wish I had" at the end of your life. I suggest to everyone, live life to the fullest — as best as you can — live while you're alive!

Ecclesiastes, chapter nine verse nine, states that a man should "live happily with the woman he loves." I *did* find love in my lifetime, for I do have a wife and child. According to this same verse, "The wife God gives you is your best reward for all your earthly toil." I read this and I fully realize, God is good to me!

Sure life has its problems and challenges — this will always be true for everybody. But God is a loving God. I suggest turning to the Bible. Again, I emphasize that reading the Bible points a person to the truths about God and life that is more beneficial than "tradition-based religion." I am writing this as a non-religious man who recognizes the Bible for what it is — God' Word of inspiration to the world.

I am confident that I would have collapsed into a state of depressed oblivion if I didn't have the Bible to turn to. I didn't come to God through any church or religious entity. I came to God because I literally found myself alone with no where else to turn. People have done wrong things to me, but I've done wrong things to people as well. I'm not writing this to make anybody feel bad or to even make myself feel good. If anything, I hope this writing raises people's consciences about their fellow human beings.

I'm not God. I cannot save the world. I cannot even save myself. I am not perfect and I cannot create perfection. I can only point to the One who has helped me — One who's been there through good and bad times.

Let us all be more cognizant of God and conscious of our fellow human beings as we travel this road called life.

- *Noel Trowers*

The Master Designer

LIVING THE CHRISTIAN LIFE is much like the making of a quilt. The analogy is particularly evident if one imagines a group of people collectively working on a large multi-colored intricate quilt. God is the Master Designer of our lives. As Christians, we are to contribute different things to the "quilt" — because we have each been given different tasks and responsibilities by God. This He has done in accordance with our individual abilities and capacities, which He also has given us.

God has assigned to each of us a different section, a different detail of the "quilt" — our role in this life. Our responsibility as Christians is to individually perform our assigned task to the best of our abilities according to the guidelines, the "pattern" given to us in God's Word — the "blueprint" for our lives. God is the Master Designer — as His children we must follow His every lead without hesitation or reservation, because He is God.

Being only small parts of the whole, we cannot, and should not try to comprehend the "entire quilt." The master plan is in the Master's hands — we can rest assured that His will is going to be done. Even as He gives us instruction that we do not understand, we as Christians should perform them readily, simply because we know that He is the Master Designer. We should realize and accept with full confidence that His guidelines are best, because He is God. He holds the Master Plan for our lives.

In conclusion, let us each "work on our individual portion of the quilt" following the Master's guidelines, just as we are to work on the portion in life that God has given us according to His Word, the guidebook for our lives. Let us thank Him for the things that He allows us to understand, and trust completely in His faithfulness for the things we do not understand. He is the Master Designer for our lives. He holds the plan, the "pattern," the "blueprint." Let us trust in Him — knowing with confidence that He will "put it all together in the end" — for His Glory. Amen!